THE FOAL IN THE WOMB

A simple illustrated account of the
events that lead to the birth of a foal

A. W. Marrable
School of Veterinary Science
University of Bristol

J. A. ALLEN
London and New York

ACKNOWLEDGEMENTS

The author and Publisher warmly thank the following persons for advice or assistance: Mrs. J. Gillard, Miss M. N. Heaver, Dr. W. A. G. Charleston, Dr. P. F. Flood, Dr. J. R. Holmes, Dr. P. G. G. Darke and Mr. R. P. Radnedge.

Printed in Malta by Interprint Ltd.

CONTENTS

1 Sexual Biology of Mare and Stallion

Every new-born foal comes from an egg that started to grow about 11 months earlier in the womb of a mare. During these prenatal months—which are known as the period of gestation—the egg, a microscopic globule weighing approximately one millionth of a gramme, develops into a foal of about 50 kilogrammes. An increase of nearly one hundred thousand millionfold! Our purpose is to look briefly but carefully into this secret part of life, because the events of pregnancy are not only of the greatest interest in themselves but a knowledge of them is necessary for that fuller understanding of equine physiology desired by serious students and lovers of horses.

Most fillies become sexually capable between 12 and 24 months after birth; the eggs are formed inside their ovaries where they are nourished in fluid-filled sacs called follicles (*Figure 1A, C*). Only a few of the very large number of eggs available in the two ovaries ever succeed in ripening, but those that do are eventually liberated by the bursting of their follicles into a shallow pit on the surface of each ovary (*Figure 1A*). This sudden process is called ovulation. Immediately after escaping, the eggs enter the funnel of a narrow tube that leads to the uterus or womb (*Figure 1A, B*). For several days before the eggs are released, the walls of the follicles synthesise a potent hormone (chemical messenger) which entering the bloodstream is carried about the mare's body making her ready and eager to accept the stallion's advances at the very time the eggs are available for fertilisation. Sexual ardour in the mare is known as "heat" or "oestrus"; the Greek word "oestrus" means "mad desire" so the chemical messenger that causes it is appropriately called an oestrogen —a producer of desire.

The accurate detection of oestrus is important to horse-breeders. A distinct change in a mare's behaviour is the earliest sign. If she is a lone animal the change may be slight, but if she can smell, hear, or see a stallion, it can be intense, persistent, and unmistakable. If he has access she will allow him to smell and bite her; she will urinate frequently and mucus will escape from the vulva. With increasing sexual excitement the mare's clitoris will erect and the vulval lips appear swollen (*Figure 1B*); she is said to "show". Long experience, patient observations, and a familiarity with individual animals favour the recognition of oestrus. The duration of heat varies, and is influenced by season, locality, breed, and the characteristics of the individual mare: the usually quoted averages are 6 and 7 days but any length between 2 and 11 days is considered normal. The intensity of desire reaches a climax near the time of ovulation, which takes place about 24 hours before the end of heat.

Let us now consider the part played by the male horse who normally becomes sexually competent in his second year. The germ cells or sperms are formed in the testes (testicles) which are accommodated in the stallion's scrotum. In a mature animal about 8000 million sperms are normally available at any one time. The sperms although individually much smaller than the eggs (*Figure 2B*) are equally important for they carry the hereditary traits of the father. One sperm and one egg must meet and combine before the egg will

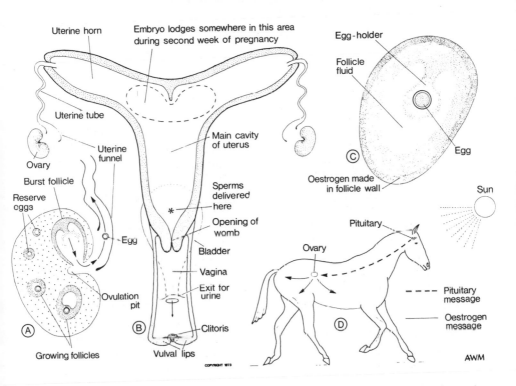

Figure 1 **A** *Internal details of mare's ovary showing egg from burst follicle entering the uterine funnel* **B** *Genital organs of mare seen from above: womb shown with heavier outline* **C** *Single ripe follicle magnified to show egg holder* **D** *Diagrammatic summary of solar and hormonal control of female sexual cycle*

start to develop into an embryo. The joining of egg and sperm is called fertilisation and for this to happen the sperms must be spurted into the mare's womb from the stallion's penis during the spasm of copulation; he is said to "cover" or "serve" the mare.

In free ranging horses living in herds, copulation is preceded by a more or less elaborate courtship. The stallion will whinny and snort; will smell and nip the mare's mane and back; and—most characteristically—will stretch head and neck high in the air whilst curling back his upper lip (the "flehmen" posture). As courtship proceeds the stallion's penis slides from its sheath and stiffens. If the mare is receptive—which she will be at the height of oestrus— the stallion will rear up and mount from behind and the penis will enter the mare's genital passage. After several thrusts the stallion lies still on the mare at which moment the semen (sperm fluid) is ejaculated into the uterus. The relaxed stallion then dismounts.

From the main chamber of the uterus the swarm of sperms ascend the meandering uterine tubes in which they meet the recently ovulated eggs or await their arrival if mating precedes ovulation (*Figure 1A, B*). It is largely a matter of chance which of the thousands of sperm that surround the egg actually enters it; but one sperm only is successful, after which the egg becomes impenetrable to the remainder which soon grow feeble and die. Fertilisation has been achieved.

2 The Breeding Cycle

Now that the essential biology of courtship and mating has been outlined, we can consider how these events link with gestation, lactation, and foaling to form the breeding or reproductive cycle.

If a mare is not mated during heat or if mated fails to conceive she loses interest in the stallion for a period of 15 to 16 days, after which she comes on heat again. This repetitive pattern of short periods of sexual zeal separated by longer placid intervals is called the oestrous cycle (*Figure 2A*); it recurs about every 21 days (6 days oestrus+15 days interval) until either the mare becomes pregnant (*Figure 2A, Mare Y*) or the mating season ends and she enters a prolonged period of sexual dormancy called anoestrus, which usually coincides with the winter (*Figure 2A, Mare X*). It must be emphasised that the model cycles we have described and illustrated are simplifications of the actual rhythms, which show many variations and irregularities especially amongst fully domesticated horses.

Highly fertile mares who become pregnant in their first season and regularly thereafter, are seldom subjected to a prolonged run of oestrous cycles; instead their lives are dominated by a sequence of annual pregnancies, so that as well as suckling a foal at foot they generally carry a foal within (*Figure 2A, Mare Y*). Eleven months is usually taken as the length of pregnancy in the mare because it is easy to remember; another popular standard is 336 days. However, the duration of gestation varies widely with the averages for different breeds ranging from 329 to 345 days, the lighter horses having the longer periods. A celebrated expert on farm animals, Professor Sir John Hammond of Cambridge University, made a special study of gestation length in a group of Welsh ponies. He found that foals conceived in March were carried as much as a month longer than those conceived in June. Thus although matings were spread through three months the consequent foalings in the following year were crowded into two bountiful months of the early summer.

About 9 days after the birth of a foal, its dam shows the foal heat at which she may again become pregnant, although frequently this does not happen until the next heat after a further 21 days or even longer delay (*Figure 2A, Mare Y*). It will be seen that an eleven-months gestation plus 9 or more days makes up a breeding cycle which closely approaches a full solar year; because of this, matings and foalings tend to occur at the same time of year and are mingled activities in herds of wild horses.

In wild or semi-wild horses it is quite obvious that the breeding cycle is closely linked with the seasons of the year. This relationship has come about during the evolution of the horse in prehistoric times and we can glimpse its biological significance by examining how seasonal and climatic changes would have affected the herds of wild horses that wandered on the great grassy plains of the Eurasian land-mass twelve thousand years ago. During the searing Northern winter all their senses and energies were fiercely engaged in scratching and nibbling survival from the scant and frozen tufts, but when the mist, snow, and ice declined in the late spring and the noon sun, day by day, climbed higher in the sky, so they began to

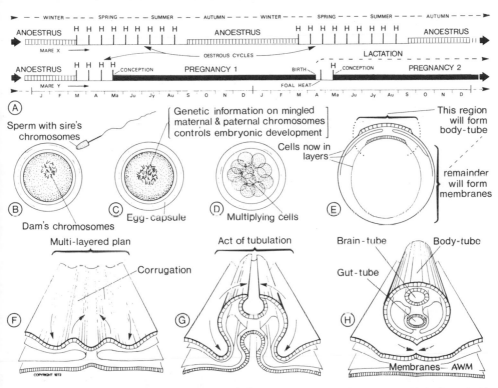

Figure 2 **A** *Diagrammatic comparison of the breeding cycles of mares X and Y through the seasons of two successive years in the Northern Temperate Zone: read from left to right: letter H stands for "heat"* **B** *Unfertilised horse egg with approaching sperm* **C** *Recently fertilised egg* **D** *Cell cluster* **E** *Many-layered conceptus: 2-3 weeks* **F, G,** *and* **H** *Perspective diagrams of 3 stages in the rolling-up of the body-tube (highly simplified): arrows show formative movements*

breed. Pregnant mares dropped their foals and freed from long burden began in a few days to show a renewed interest in the eager stallions. After the rigour of winter, soft new grass, shooting in response to the strengthening sunlight and vernal rain, was keenly sought by growing foals, lactating mares, and lean stallions.

Modern research has shown that the primary link between the breeding and seasonal cycles is the change in the direction and intensity of the light rays falling on our Planet as it spins and swings round our Star. The quickening of sexual interest in the spring is a sensitive response to the increasing sunlight and shortening darkness. In the mare the main physiological steps are probably as follows: sunlight collected by the eye is measured by the brain rather in the manner of a photographer's light meter; as soon as a certain solar strength or duration is recorded the brain instructs the nearby pituitary organ to release into the blood a master hormone, which swiftly flowing to the ovaries triggers the growth and ripening of the follicles (*Figure 1D*). Then the swelling follicles in their turn liberate the messenger oestrogens which start up the cycles of appropriate sexual behaviour (*Figures 1C, D & 2A*).

Naturally the seasons occur at different times of the year in various parts of the World and so depending on the geographical location the breeding activities of the horse occupy different calendar months. For example in the North Temperate Zone ($23\frac{1}{2}°$ to $63\frac{1}{2}°$ N) mating and foaling predominate in April, May and June; but, as Professor R. M. Butterfield has shown, in Australia at latitude 35° S, the corresponding months are September, October and November. In the

8

Torrid Zones on either side of the equator ($0°$ to $23\frac{1}{2}°$ N and $0°$ to $23\frac{1}{2}°$ S), where sunlight is more uniform from month to month, horses breed throughout the year.

Fully domesticated horses have been subjected to unnatural conditions of management for thousands of years; darkened stables in the day, lighted stables at night, equitation, selective mating, sexual isolations, and special diets, are only some of the influences that have almost certainly altered their reproductive habits. The supposition that artificial lighting can affect the oestrous cycle was confirmed experimentally in 1946 by Dr. John Burkhardt who, working at Cambridge in England ($52°$ N) was able to "shift" the mating season of stabled New Forest ponies by exposing them to long periods of electric lighting during the winter—a time when they are usually sexually placid. He succeeded in bringing forward their first heats, normally seen in April, by about two months. Burkhardt's studies are in good agreement with those of the distinguished Japanese scientist Professor Y. Nishikawa who using Korean mares achieved similar results in Japan ($35°$ N) in 1950.

It is appropriate to mention at this point the work of the Newmarket veterinary surgeon Peter Rossdale who has made special studies on the behavioural aspects of reproduction in Thoroughbreds. It is possible, he argues, that some of the difficulties encountered in breeding bloodstock are due to the highly artificial environment in which modern horse mating takes place. He suggests that a detailed study of the sexual behaviour of free-ranging horses would yield information of value in practical stud management.

3 The Potent Egg

For most of us the word "egg" means the hen's egg—a highly nutritive food consisting of hard shell, clear albumen, and an orange yolk; the whole thing weighing between 50 and 60 grams (about 2 ounces). Compared with this familiar culinary object the thought of a horse's egg is strange and perhaps slightly amusing.

Eggs of fishes, frogs, snakes, and birds, have been known for thousands of years but mammalian eggs are comparatively recent discoveries. It was not until 1827 that a German embryologist K. E. von Baer discovered the human egg and the equine egg was first described in 1939 by Professor E. C. Amoroso and his colleagues working at the Royal Veterinary College, London.

The newly-fertilised horse egg measures between 0·1 and 0·2 milli-metres in diameter; six of them placed in contact along a line span only one millimetre. A horse egg can just be discerned by the unaided human eye, but when a fresh specimen is examined through a microscope it is seen as a beautifully-spheroidal bead of protoplasmic jelly surrounded by a transparent capsule (*Figure 2C*). The smallness of the egg is at first a matter for surprise; we ask how such a mighty animal as a horse can arise from so little an object? And why does the hen, which is much smaller than a horse, have a larger egg? The chief reason for the great difference in size is that the horse egg contains hardly any stored food such as makes up the bulk of the hen's egg. And the reason why the horse egg holds no needless food deposits is because the embryo it gives rise to will receive a steady supply of nourishment from its mother's uterus throughout gestation.

If the equine egg holds but little food, what then does it contain? The answer is the hereditary information and synthetic mechanism which models the materials supplied by the mare into the familiar shape and substance of the new-born foal. For unlike food, information can be stored in very little space, especially if it is organised as a code. The coded genetic information in a fertilised horse egg is carried on 64 microscopic threads—the chromosomes—clustered at the centre of the egg (*Figure 2C*). Half of the chromosomes—exactly 32—were already in the egg before fertilisation and they carry the maternal characters to be inherited by the future foal; the other 32, carrying the paternal hereditary contribution, were delivered by the fertilising sperm (*Figure 2B*). Thus it should be noted, both sire and dam supply chromosomal information to control the embryonic formation of their offspring, who in this way receives inborn characteristics from both parents.

Not only does the fertilised egg contain all the necessary biological instructions for the fabrication of a foal, it also contains the information required to organise the vital membranes that harbour the embryonic foal during its sojourn in the uterus. These membranes appear at an early stage and grow rapidly to achieve a close contact with the lining of the uterus; they play a major role in the protection of the embryo and are essential for the efficient passage of foodstuffs from the uterine lining to the embryo. We shall return to these structures later and meanwhile it suffices to point out that following the birth of the foal they are cast out as the afterbirth.

We end this section by introducing the useful word "conceptus". The conceptus is the whole structure arising from the egg: it thus comprises the membranes and fluids as well as the growing body of the future animal.

4 The Body-tube Appears

Immediately after fertilisation the previously dormant egg becomes intensely active; a ferment of biochemical change is started and embryological development begins. Soon the egg divides into two smaller cells each of which divides again within a few hours to give a total of four. Multiplication of cells once begun continues speedily, the initial pattern of increase being a progression of the form 1 2 4 8 16 32 64 128 256 and so on. As the cell population mounts through the thousands into the ten thousands and beyond, the pace of multiplication slackens but by no means stops. In this way the egg undergoes an orderly transformation into a multitude of small manoeuvrable units that are the fundamental building blocks of the animal body. At first they form a compact cluster still within the egg capsule (*Figure 2D*), but by the end of the second week of pregnancy the capsule has been lost and the cells have reformed into a hollow, multi-layered ball which has swollen to about 2 centimetres in diameter as a result of taking in fluids and nutriment from the lining of the womb (*Figure 2E*).

As early as the start of the third week of development the beginnings of the body of the future horse can be located as a specialised region in the wall of the layered sac (*Figure 2E*); not of course as a microscopic facsimile of the mature animal but in the form of a plan. It must be emphasised that, unlike an architect's plan or an engineer's blueprint on a single sheet, the lay-out of the embryonic horse is on several superimposed sheets of living cells (*Figure 2F*) which far from being disposable are actually incorporated into the tissues of the growing animal!

Now, in the middle of the third week, comes the most dramatic phase of development as the layered plan is rolled up by invisible forces to form the main body cylinder; at the same time, by complex infoldings, a tubular gut, a hollow brain-tube, and many other organs are laid down. A simplified version of this remarkable act of "tubulation" is illustrated in *Figures 2F, 2G & 2H*. Tubulation takes three consecutive days to form an embryonic body 5 millimetres long.

5 We Recognise the Foetal Foal

When first formed the body-tube is nearly straight but within a few hours it becomes notably bent and by the end of the third week of gestation definite regions of the body can be recognised (*Figure 3A*). The most obvious part is the head, known by the presence of brain swellings, the beginnings of upper and lower jaws, and the first signs of eyes and ears. By the end of the fourth week the head is connected to the sturdy barrel of the trunk by a strongly-curved neck and the thin belly wall is swollen by the heart and liver—vital organs that are already working and occupying much of the body cavity. There is a tapering tail. Smooth flanges on either side of the body above the heart swelling can be identified as fore-limb buds; after a few more days the hind-limb buds appear (*Figure 3B*).

As the embryo enters the fifth week of gestation it has acquired most of the fundamentals of mammalian organisation: a large brain, a four-chambered heart, lungs, a larynx, an ear-flap, and not least, mammary glands, the structures which give this class of animals its name—Mammalia. Yet the embryo still does not look like a horse and is not very different in appearance from comparable stages in the development of other mammals such as pigs, cattle, and sheep. However, by the sixth week, each limb develops a distinct taper with a single main digit which shows the embryo to be indubitably a member of the horse family. All four limbs have now elongated so that they protrude beyond the swollen abdomen; shoulder and hip swellings are easily visible and the angles of knee, hock, and stifle may just be detected (*Figure 3C*).

It is convenient at this point to explain the use of the words "embryo" and "foetus". Any stage of development from a fertilised egg to an animal about to be born may be correctly called an embryo; but when a mammalian embryo has developed enough to be recognisable as the kind of animal it is going to be, it is often called a foetus. On that basis we can see that the foetal period in the horse begins about the sixth week of pregnancy.

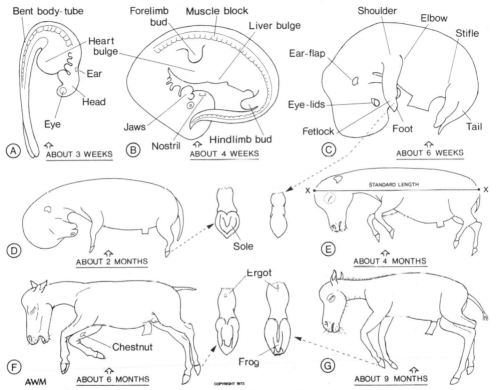

Figure 3 **A–G** *Sequence of horse embryos and foetuses of increasing prenatal age. The ground or bearing surface of the foot is shown at 6 weeks, 2 months, 6 months and 9 months gestation. The line X–X in* **E** *shows the standard length referred to in the growth table inside the back cover*

6 The Foetus Matures

By the end of the second prenatal month, the foetus not only possesses definite equine structures but has become horse-like in profile and general proportions (*Figure 3D*). Let us specify some of the changes that have taken place in the seventh and eighth weeks. The neck is longer and the head is gradually lifting to a nobler carriage. The nostrils have assumed their characteristic position and shape, whilst eyelids have grown over the bulging eyeballs, each of which is already equipped with retina and lens. Triangular ear-flaps cover the openings of the ear canals. Shoulder and hip are shaping and the buttock is filling with propulsive muscle. Elbow, knee, stifle, and hock are recognisable; fetlocks and hoofs are formed. There is no doubt we now have a miniature horse; semi-transparent, and fragile, but unmistakeable and only about 5 centimetres long.

By the beginning of the third month the major internal organs are well-established and, with few exceptions, have reached their final positions in the foetal body. And yet there are still nine long months to go before birth! These are the months of maturation; of growth in size and weight accompanied by detailed cellular and biochemical organisation. Some especially interesting aspects of this long preparation for postnatal life are discussed in a following section but meanwhile we summarise the more obvious external changes which take place.

By the end of the third month the head and neck have attained their normal posture and the eyelids have sealed over the prominent eyeballs (*Figure 3E*). Curved ear-flaps are conspicuous. Muscular contours are visible beneath the translucent skin and the general conformation can be cautiously assessed. A coronary line clearly separates the pale yellow and ivory hoof from the rest of each limb; in the developing hoof, the wall, sole, and frog are recognisable.

By the sixth month the proportions of the foetus are as close to those of the adult horse as they are at any stage of prenatal life (*Figure 3F*); from this time on, the limbs grow somewhat faster than the rest of the body to give the stilty legs of the foal. The skin is thickening and is much less transparent. Bristles are appearing on upper and lower lips and there is fine hair on the muzzle, the chin, and around the eyelids. The longer hairs of mane and tail are just appearing; ergots and chestnuts have developed on all four limbs.

By nine months gestation a coat of fine body-hair has developed. There are sturdy whiskers on throat, chin, and muzzle and the hair of the mane is several millimetres long. A short switch is forming at the end of the tail. On the ground surface of each foot, a pad of swollen horn has obscured frog and sole. As a result of their un-trammelled growth in the warm amniotic fluid, the developing hoofs are longer and more pointed than those of the adult whose lower surfaces are continuously worn away by contact with the ground. And the foetal hoofs are certainly much softer and therefore unlikely to damage the womb and foetal membranes during pregnancy or at parturition. Apart from thickening of the coat the external appearance of the foetal foal changes little between this stage and the time of birth at eleven months.

In this brief description of equine development we have deliberately concentrated on the remarkable and ceaseless changes of shape. But of course as the embryo gets older and more complex it also increases rapidly in size and weight. Some numerical data illustrating this growth in bulk are for convenient reference printed inside the back cover.

7 Structure of the Foetal Package

Those parts of the early multi-layered conceptus (*Figure 2E*) that are not used to form the body cylinder give rise to the membranes which complete the embryonic package. The arrangement of the membranes about mid-way through the second month is shown in *Figure 4A*. The innermost membrane, called the allanto-amnion, contains a watery fluid (amniotic fluid) in which the foetus is suspended. Lying below the foetal belly is a membranous bag called the yolk sac; the name is misleading because in the horse it never contains any substance like the yolk of a hen's egg. Foetus, amnion, and yolk sac are all enclosed in an outermost membrane with the cumbrous technical name of allanto-chorion. The space between the inner and outer membranes is filled with a second voluminous watery fluid (allantoic fluid). The surface of the package—which at this stage consists mostly of allanto-chorion with a small patch of yolk-sac wall is in close contact with the lining of the womb.

By the beginning of the third month the membranes have simplified, because the yolk-sac grows very little and is squashed, shrunken, and displaced, so that the outer wall of the conceptus is eventually made up only of allanto-chorion (*Figure 4B*). Apart from a steady growth in size the general structure of the package then remains unchanged until birth—that is for about the last three quarters of gestation.

The foetus is connected to both inner and outer membranes by the flexible umbilical cord (navel cord). It passes from the navel through the inner fluid, penetrates the inner membrane and continues across the outer fluid to the outer membrane. The cord contains the vital umbilical arteries and veins that run to and from the surface of the package (*Figure 5B*) as well as the diminished remnant of the yolk sac (*Figure 4B*).

Embedded in the outer membrane is a delicate tracery of minute blood-vessels, called capillaries, which are supplied and drained by the robust umbilical vessels. In early pregnancy when these capillaries are few in number and well-spaced, the outer membrane is transparent so that the foetus, surrounded by the inner membrane, is clearly visible. Later, as the blood vessels increase in size, number, and complexity, the surface becomes a rich and opaque carmine due to the presence in the now more densely-packed capillaries of a larger quantity of circulating blood. The surface of the outer membrane is mainly smooth at first (*Figure 4A*) but by two months gestation fine processes called villi (singular is villus) grow out from the membrane and push into the uterine lining (*Figure 4B*).

8 How the Embryo gets Food and Oxygen

We have shown that the horse egg is very small and unlike the yolky eggs of birds and reptiles contains hardly any stored food. It is therefore clear that all the additional material needed to make the foetal foal must be supplied by the mother during gestation and our present purpose is to explain how and when it is provided.

We begin with the commonplace observation that the pregnant mare in the wild state feeds mainly on grass—its leaves, stems, seeds, and sometimes its roots. Once in the mouth, the herbage is ground by the formidable back teeth, mixed with saliva and swallowed into the stomach from whence, after further mixing and chemical attack by gastric juices, the partly digested mass is squeezed into the intestinal coils. By this stage, much of the food has been reduced to molecules so small and mobile that their high-speed random swarming (helped by special absorbing mechanisms) carries them sooner or later through the lining of the gut into the swiftly-flowing blood of the intestinal capillaries. As the enriched maternal blood circulates through the mare's body, her organs and tissues draw on the billions of nutritive molecules; and the pregnant uterus with its lavish blood supply (*Figure 5B*) is well able to take a share which is rapidly made available to the foetal package where it presses against the internal surface of the womb.

Let us briefly consider embryonic respiration. Obviously the embryo cannot breathe air while living in the uterus surrounded by fluid! Yet it uses oxygen in the same way as adult tissue for the

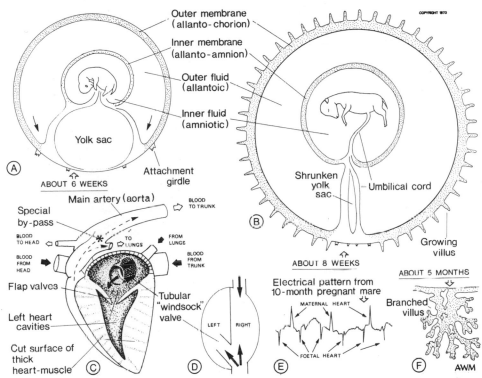

Figure 4 **A** *Embryonic package at 6 weeks gestation* **B** *Embryonic package with sprouting outer membrane at 8 weeks gestation* **C** *Heart of a horse foetus (about 6 months): wall of left heart cavity opened to show flap valves and middle partition with "windsock" valve* **D** *Diagram of cross-section through same foetal heart seen from above: showing how blood can pass through middle wall of foetal heart by way of tubular valve (highly simplified)* **E** *Electrocardiogram from pregnant mare (based on Holmes, J. R. & Darke, P. G. G. 1968 Vet. Rec.* **82**, *651)* **F** *Branching villus*

release of essential energy. Fortunately the embryo's needs are amply satisfied by transference of oxygen from the mother's blood in the uterine capillaries to those of the outer package membrane (*Figure 5A*). Of course, the oxygen for the foetus is taken in by the mare's lungs along with her own requirements in the first place and so, as with food, the provisioning of the foetus is indirect.

As pregnancy advances the surface of the swelling conceptus is bathed and sustained by a rich secretion released at the inner surface of the womb by a multitude of glands embedded in the uterine wall; chemical analysis shows that the so-called uterine "milk" is about 80% water, the remainder being a mixture of nutritious substances of which protein is present in greatest amount. As well as providing a liquid food for easy absorption at the surface of the embryonic sac, the "milk" lubricates the delicate membranes.

By the third week of gestation a network of blood vessels has developed in the outermost membrane of the swelling conceptus which is held gently but firmly against the uterine lining by the accumulating embryonic fluids. In this way the smallest branches of the embryonic circulation are laid against the equally intricate mesh of maternal capillaries that lies immediately below the uterine surface. It is important to realise that the maternal and foetal blood vessels are never directly connected to each other but are merely in intimate proximity; so close however that nutrient molecules and oxygen move with ease from maternal to embryonic capillaries in one direction while waste products pass from embryo to mother in reverse (*Figure 5A*). Once the in-going molecules have been transferred to the allanto-chorionic vessels they are promptly carried to the embryonic body by passing through the large veins in the umbilical cord (*Figure 5B*). After being distributed to various parts of the embryo, the blood, now with diminished food and oxygen but laden with carbon dioxide, is returned via the umbilical arteries to be refreshed at the package surface.

If the uterus is opened surgically during the first two or three months of pregnancy, the conceptus falls by its own weight from the uterine wall; later than this the membranes adhere and can only be removed by pulling. This stronger attachment (which is maintained until near the end of pregnancy) is achieved by the sprouting growth of the initially finger-like allanto-chorionic processes into tree-like forms (*Figures 4B, F*) that fit snugly into branching pits in the spongy uterine wall (*Figure 5A, B*). The region of interlocking processes and pits is known as the placenta—the mediatory organ in which molecular exchanges between mother and foetus take place. As well as facilitating the exchange of simple nutrients and waste products, the placenta acts as a selective filter preventing the passage of substances that although normal and acceptable in the mother's blood are harmful to the embryo and vice-versa. That the placenta is highly efficient can scarcely be in doubt, for during the last month of gestation the foetal foal gains about one third of a kilogramme ($\frac{3}{4}$ lb) in weight per day.

9 Colt or Filly?

After caring for a pregnant mare through many long months, one of the excitements of at last seeing the newborn foal is that of knowing its sex. Important decisions depend on whether it be a colt or a filly: its value to the owner; whether to sell or to keep; and in the case of a colt, to geld (castrate) or leave entire. The sex of a young animal undoubtedly influences its future.

In order to understand how the sex of an animal is established we need first to consider some events that precede conception, then fertilisation itself, and finally the growth of the foetal genital organs.

The essential facts are that whereas a mare makes only one kind of egg a stallion produces two sorts of germ-cells known as male-forming and female-forming sperms. Both kinds of sperm are produced in equal numbers, which are randomly and inextricably mixed in the ejaculated semen, so that the unfertilised egg has an even chance of meeting either kind after copulation. If the egg is first entered by a male-forming sperm it will develop into a colt; if by a female-forming sperm it will give rise to a filly.

It is of interest to note in passing that male-forming and female-forming sperm show no obvious differences under the microscope. The existence of two kinds of sperm has been deduced from early stages in the formation of sperm in the testes and slight differences in the chromosome patterns of mare and stallion.

Although the future sex of a horse is determined at fertilisation, no outward differences between male and female embryos can be seen during the first month of development. It is true that the beginnings of sexual structures appear but they are present in all embryos and are only modified later to form male or female organs. The most obvious example is the genital hillock which develops between the hind-legs during the fourth week; in the sixth week of gestation, it begins to be transformed into a tubular penis in the male embryo, whereas in the female it remains as a non-tubular clitoris. From this time on, the sex of an embryo or foetus is easily recognised.

The internal sex organs, which begin to appear about the third week of pregnancy are initially similar in all embryos whether genetically male or female; soon however they develop along different pathways so that by the end of the first month either testes or ovaries are present in the abdominal cavities.

In the case of fillies the ovaries remain in the abdomen, but in colt foetuses a slow migration of the testes into the scrotum begins about the third month of gestation, with the testes actually entering the scrotum either just before, during, or just after birth. Quite frequently one or both testes fail to descend properly and are either retained in the abdomen or become lodged in the abdominal wall near the groin. An adult horse having this condition is known as a rig or cryptorchid (a Greek word meaning "hidden testis"). Although an undescended testis does not produce sperm, the horse may still show stallion-like behaviour. To produce a proper gelding from a rig it is necessary to remove the undescended abdominal testis or testes, as well as any that are scrotal in position.

10 Life in the Womb

During the first few months of pregnancy the embryo is suspended, silent and still, in the warm darkness of the amniotic fluid. Towards the middle of gestation the foetal muscles develop the ability to contract and irregular head and limb movements may occur. However it seems that prolonged and violent activity is generally suppressed for most of gestation, probably to prevent damage to the membranes and uterus and to minimise the production of heat by the foetus—heat that must eventually be dissipated by the mare. Powerful and persistent movements of the foetal body and limbs start up in the few weeks before birth; these movements can sometimes be seen and felt in the mare's flank.

Although the early embryo is delicately gelatinous and has as yet no rigid skeleton, it is so cushioned from blows and shocks by the surrounding foetal fluids that the lightly pregnant mare can trot, canter, gallop, and even jump without harming her unborn offspring. This must be considered a significant biological advantage for a grazing animal in the wild. The plentiful package fluids not only give buoyant support to the soft embryo but also provide a "reserved" living space into which it can grow without touching the inside of the uterus or being pressed by the writhing of the gut.

As gestation proceeds, various organs and systems start to function in a well-ordered sequence at suitable levels of activity. This gradually increasing foetal vitality relieves some of the strain on the mare's own tissues and exercises the growing organs in preparation for the sudden demands to be made on them by the newborn foal.

There can be no doubt that the heart and blood vessels are both structurally and functionally the most precocious organs. The embryonic heart begins to beat and circulate blood as marvellously early as the third week after conception when the whole embryo is only about 1 centimetre long; once started, it never stops until death! The heart is proportionately larger in the embryo than in the adult, but that is not surprising because in addition to pumping blood around the developing body, the embryonic heart circulates blood through the vital package membranes well beyond the body's confines (*Figure 5B*).

Whilst pumping, the heart generates an electrical rhythm which can be picked up with a sensitive receiver, amplified, and displayed as a graph called an electrocardiogram. In the pregnant mare, from about 5 months gestation onwards, a foetal electrocardiogram can also be detected and compared with that of the maternal heart; such a recording, made by Drs. J. Holmes and P. Darke of Bristol University, is shown in *Figure 5E*. A similar study of Percheron mares at Sapporo in Japan showed that during the last two months of gestation the foetal heart-rate varied from 84 to 114 beats per second whilst the maternal heart ranged between 42 and 78. The foetal heart pumped nearly twice as fast as that of its mother.

Very sturdy blood vessels running from the heart to the lungs are laid down at an early stage in readiness for the voluminous supply of blood suddenly required by the lungs at the instant the first breath is taken at birth. But since the foetus gets its oxygen

27

through the placenta, its lungs although growing are not yet working and hence for the time being need only a modest circulation. Consequently, in order to prevent the foetal lungs being overloaded with blood and yet allow the necessary steady development of robust pulmonary vessels, a special escape artery is provided in which some of the blood by-passes the lungs and is diverted to the trunk (*Figure 4C*). In addition, a hole with a tubular "windsock" valve is provided in the wall between the two sides of the heart. This allows blood to flow from right to left until balance is reached and the growing heart is able to beat in a symmetrically weighted condition (*Figure 4C & D*). At birth the lungs expand and take up the task of oxygenating the foal's blood; they now require the fullest possible blood supply, and this is promptly achieved by the permanent closure of the now obsolete valve and by-pass.

Turning to the developing digestive system, we find that although no solid food is available the foetal foal probably swallows amniotic fluid from time to time thereby exercising its oesophagus, stomach, and intestines in preparation for suckling. Despite the watery diet a surprising amount of material is found in the foetal gut! It includes scales and hairs from the foal's skin, surplus cells worn from the lining of the gut, and green bile pigment. The contents of the stomach and first coils of intestine are semi-fluid, but in the mid-gut they become pasty and towards the anus there is sufficient muscular activity to mould the excrement into pellets. The foetuses of some animals are known to defaecate *in utero* and this may occur in the foal, but normally the foetal excrement (meconium) is retained

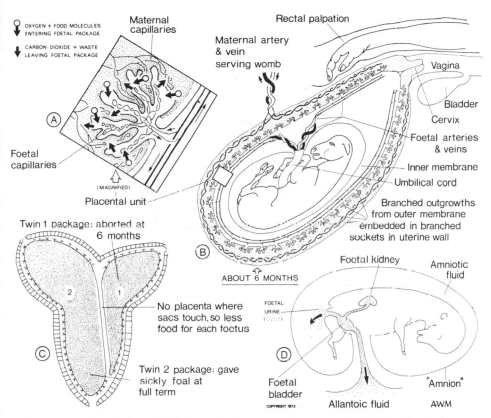

Figure 5 **A** *Detail of magnified placental unit: maternal tissue is stippled* **B** *Womb of mare at about 6 months gestation: the foetal circulation is separate from that of the mother: veterinary surgeon's hand in rectum can examine pregnancy by touch* **C** *Competition between twin packages* **D** *Production and storage of foetal urine*

Within the figure:

OXYGEN + FOOD MOLECULES ENTERING FOETAL PACKAGE

CARBON DIOXIDE + WASTE LEAVING FOETAL PACKAGE

Maternal capillaries

Maternal artery & vein serving womb

Rectal palpation

Vagina

Bladder

Cervix

Foetal arteries & veins

Inner membrane

Umbilical cord

Branched outgrowths from outer membrane embedded in branched sockets in uterine wall

Foetal capillaries

(MAGNIFIED)

Placental unit

(A)

(B)

ABOUT 6 MONTHS

Twin 1 package: aborted at 6 months

No placenta where sacs touch, so less food for each foetus

Twin 2 package: gave sickly foal at full term

(C)

Foetal kidney

Amniotic fluid

FOETAL URINE

Foetal bladder

Allantoic fluid

"Amnion"

AWM

(D)

COPYRIGHT 1973

throughout gestation to be evacuated a day or two after birth

Filtration of blood by the kidneys starts in the horse embryo by the end of the second month of gestation. The foetal urine passes to the developing bladder whence it is squeezed into the inner package fluid (amniotic) through the usual channels, or into the outer fluid (allantoic) through a special tube in the umbilical cord which is sealed-off when the cord breaks at birth (*Figure 5D*).

During the first third of gestation the outer allantoic fluid is transparent but from then onwards becomes a cloudy yellow-brown as it is contaminated with foetal urine. A single white or yellow-brown flattened pellet is normally found in the allantoic fluid from about the third month; roundish at first and about 1 centimetre across, it persists, gradually getting larger and more oval until it may attain 10 centimetres or more by the time it is found amongst the discarded membranes after the birth of the foal. This curious object was known to Aristotle and is still called by the ancient Greek name "hippomane". There is a good deal of folklore associated with hippomanes. A Twelfth Century bestiary says: "At birth a love charm is delivered with the foal, which they carry on their foreheads. It is of a tawny colour, similar to a dried fig". A fanciful German rural name for a hippomane is "Fohlenbrot" which means foal's bread—suggesting erroneously that it is used as food by the foetal foal. However, Dr. J. M. King has shown recently that a hippomane is probably formed by sedimentation of cloudy allantoic material to the bottom of the foetal package where it is enlarged by new layers settling out during the rest of gestation.

11 Is the Mare in Foal?

Reliable pregnancy diagnosis is obviously of great value to owners and breeders since the future of both dam and foal can be more sensibly planned. Various methods have been advocated down the centuries, some of them being of very doubtful validity such as the following method described in "The Experienced Farrier or Farring Compleated" published in the Seventeenth Century: "To know whether your mare be with foal or not: If you pour a Spoonful of cold Vinegar or Water into her Ear, if she shake only her Head, it is a sign she is with Foal; but if she shake her Head, Body and all, then it is a sign she is not with Foal"

The irregularity of the mare's sexual physiology makes diagnosis in the early months rather difficult and uncertain. If a mare having been covered fails to conceive, she may return to service about two weeks later or she may enter a sexually dormant state which can be mistaken for pregnancy. And on the other hand, there are well-known cases of mares who although already pregnant nevertheless show signs of heat and will stand for the stallion.

Before continuing, it is necessary to stress that modern techniques of pregnancy testing are normally matters for the veterinary surgeon. However, others interested in horses can undoubtedly benefit from understanding the biological principles involved.

The foremost method is known as rectal examination. If *Figure 5B* is consulted it will be seen that the last part of the large intestine—called the rectum—lies just above and slightly behind the womb.

The wall of the rectum is relatively insensitive and will stretch enormously so that a clean, well-lubricated hand passed through the mare's anus for a distance of about 35 centimetres (say from wrist to elbow) is able to feel the position and size of the womb and ovaries through the thickness of the flabby intestinal wall. Gentleness, sensitive fingers, and considerable practice, are needed for correct diagnosis. Using this technique, a few highly-skilled practitioners have been able to detect pregnancy in the third week, but positive diagnosis more usually awaits the fifth and sixth weeks, and for the less experienced may not be possible until the third month.

A close look at the interior of the vagina with the help of an illuminating tube is another method which requires scrupulous observation and acquired skill to detect the slight changes in the colour and stickiness of the vaginal lining that take place during heat and pregnancy. Greater accuracy can be gained from microscopic examination of vaginal mucus taken with a soft paint brush, and although there are difficulties of interpretation the method is said to give 95 % correct results from the beginning of the fourth month.

There are also important biochemical tests, because as a result of pregnancy the physiology of the mare gradually changes and both she and her foetus make certain hormones in amounts not produced in the non-pregnant state. One kind of hormone appears in the maternal blood from the second to the fifth month of gestation and another kind in her urine from the third month until birth. If these can be detected they show that the mare is pregnant. Specimens of blood and urine must be collected and sent to scientific laboratories whose analysts are able to provide results by post in a few days or by telephone in a few hours.

Finally we mention a means of pregnancy detection based on the physical principle that an ultrasonic beam of short-wave, high-frequency energy striking a moving fluid is reflected back at an altered frequency—a phenomenon known as the Doppler effect. Thus, using a specially designed electronic instrument, the foetal and maternal pulse-rates can be detected and compared. Employing this method the Scottish veterinarian Andrew Fraser has shown that the equine foetal pulse can be consistently detected from about three months gestation until near the time of birth.

12 Death in the Womb

It sometimes happens that a mare thought to be firmly pregnant at the fifth week fails to complete her gestation and eventually returns to heat without producing a foal; in many of these cases spontaneous abortion has probably occurred but escaped observation. Although by no means the sole cause of the much-lamented low fertility of domesticated horses, death of the foal in the womb certainly contributes regularly to the total wastage.

This costly problem has been known for many years and as long ago as 1896 Lord Arthur Cecil consulted the distinguished Edinburgh naturalist, Professor James Cossar Ewart about "so many mares breaking service". Ewart—influenced by this discussion—

subsequently made a brilliant biological study of the problem. His main findings were published in a brochure—now rare—entitled *A Critical Period in the Development of the Horse.* Ewart showed that between 5 and 8 weeks into pregnancy there is a delicate re-organisation of the package membranes during which the blood vessels of the allantois are substituted for those of the yolk-sac (*Figures 4A, B*) as the principal nutritive pathways for the embryo. He argued that this delicate process would temporarily weaken the anchorage of the conceptus to the lining of the uterus so making the whole system especially susceptible to abortion. It is quite clear then, that mares in early pregnancy require careful handling: sudden changes of food, environment, and companions, should be mini-mised; a general serenity of management should be the aim. Un-fortunately, apart from these rules—which are no more than common sense suggests—no fundamental solution or practical treatment of the problem sprang from Professor Ewart's work. However, there has been a recent revival of interest in these matters and Drs. W. R. Allen and R. M. Moor have made studies of the first importance at Cambridge. They have provided strong evidence that during early pregnancy a "sample" of foetal cells migrate from the package and become implanted in the wall of the womb; once established they produce a hormone, known as PMSG, which possibly helps the mare maintain her pregnancy. This excellent research is still in progress and will no doubt yield further exciting results.

Stallions at stud are frequently advertised with the proviso "no foal, no fee" although from what we have just written it can be seen that pregnancy may fail despite a successful fertilisation. Nevertheless, it may not be concluded from this that the stallion is necessarily fault-free, and in general it is not possible to accurately attribute blame to either or both parents in our present state of knowledge. Moreover, it should be recognised that spontaneous abortion may act as a natural safeguard preventing hazardous gestations or the birth of biologically undesirable foals.

In the horse there are at least three kinds of prenatal deaths which for convenient reference may be called resorption, expulsion, and mummification. Resorption has been most precisely described by Dr. C. H. van Niekerk, the South African veterinary scientist. In this case, a very young embryo, approaching a month old, dies, degenerates, and dissolves—the products of the dissolution being gradually absorbed by the lining of the womb. Van Niekerk noted a correlation between such resorptions and malnutrition in mares feeding on the veld in the early Spring—normally a dry period. Mares suffering this kind of abortion generally come into season again 60 to 80 days after first service, but Van Niekerk succeeded in shortening this period in some cases by removing the residues of the dead conceptus. There can be no doubting the reality of expulsive abortion for during F. T. Day's well-known studies on equine reproduction he noted several instances of quite small embryos (about 3 weeks) being found in the vaginal passage. Records of larger foetuses thrown out at various stages throughout pregnancy are recorded only too often. Mummification is the more or less prolonged retention in the womb of a dead and dried-up foetal package. Some authorities deny its occurrence in the mare but although this may be so for singleton foals it certainly happens in many twin pregnancies.

13 Twins

It is not uncommon for several eggs to be released from the mare's ovaries during a single heat; but in most cases only one is fertilised and starts to develop, while the remainder degenerate. However in about four cases in every hundred pregnancies, two eggs are fertilised and begin parallel developments as twin embryos. It can be said immediately that their expectation of life is low since only about one in a hundred such foals survive until birth and many of these perish after they are born.

As with children, there are two kinds of twins. Identical twins develop by the splitting of one fertilised egg; since their embryonic development is controlled by the same genetic information they are necessarily the same sex—either both are female or both are male. Fraternal twins come from separately fertilised eggs and because their development is controlled by different genetic information three combinations of sex are possible: one can be a male and its twin female; or both can be female; or both be male. Most equine twins that have been sufficiently studied have proved to be two-egg twins; but of course split-egg twins are still possible.

Professor Vandeplassche, the eminent Belgian veterinary scientist, has made a special study of equine fraternal twins. He considers that the eggs usually settle one in each horn of the womb, either they come from different ovaries or, if from the same ovary, one egg crosses to the other side. In those cases where twins survive beyond ten months gestation, birth takes place at the usual time. Vandeplassche thinks it probable that twins of draught mares do better than others, presumably because the larger uterus is able to supply more easily the needs of two foetuses—needs which are very considerable during the second half of gestation. It is relevant in this connection to recall the famous experiments of Sir John Hammond and Dr. Arthur Walton who by crossing a Shire Mare with a Shetland stallion and a Shetland mare with a Shire stallion neatly demonstrated that the size of the mother can markedly affect the size of her offspring. Although the resulting foals were both Shetland-Shire crosses, the larger mother gave a considerably larger foal. Thus the small size of the womb of the Shetland dam limited the nutrition she was able to supply through the placenta and hence the growth of the foetus and the size of the foal.

Prenatal death of one or both foetal twin foals has been reported at nearly all stages of gestation. It is possible that the prompt death of one conceptus increases the chances of survival for its womb-mate but in later pregnancy the presence of a large dead foetus is a severe hazard for the live foal and also the mare. Generally the dead foetus becomes mummified within the package membranes and its presence only realised when it is found in the afterbirth of its twin. The fundamental cause of death seems to be due to the two sets of package membranes competing for the succulent and life-giving inner surface of the womb (*Figure 5C*). In so doing they interfere with each other's growth, the membranes become deranged, and one or both sacs receive insufficient food—this produces foetal stunting and frequently death with mummification. When twin foals survive it is not surprising to find that they are frequently unequal in size and usually smaller than singletons.

14 The Foal is Set Free

Birth is the climax of gestation for both mother and foetus. On the part of the mare an exhausting effort is needed to release the living burden of pregnancy; on the part of the foal there is the risk of the birth process and the stimulating change from the moist warmth of the womb to the chill of the air. One of the earliest reliable signs that the time of birth draws near is the swelling and tensing of the udder that occurs from 3 to 6 weeks before foaling. In most mares, droplets of the special early milk called colostrum leak from the udder and coagulate upon the nipple from 6 to 48 hours before birth begins; a phenomenon popularly known as "waxing".

The technical name for birth is parturition, a word derived from the Latin *parturire*, which means to bear or to be in labour. Normal parturition is a continuous natural process which is divided into three stages for ease of reference and description. As the first or preparatory stage begins the mare becomes restless, flicks her tail, kicks her belly, and may straddle her hind legs. Sweating at shoulder and flank suggests that labour has started. Meanwhile a birth canal is being prepared by muscular relaxation of the uterine neck and vagina to form a wide passage for foetal delivery (*Figure 6A*). The muscle of the uterus now squeezes the foetal package with periodic but relentless spasms which give rise to labour pains. It will be remembered that in the majority of cases the foetal foal has been lying upside down in the last months of pregnancy (*Figure 5B*). But now, as uterine activity increases, the foetus is swiftly rotated so that its back is uppermost—an astonishing manoeuvre, which Japanese scientists have skilfully shown may take as little as 18 seconds (*Figure 6A, B, C*). Foetal rotation is an important preparation for smooth delivery and it is possible that when a mare rolls on her back during labour she is trying to provoke or assist the turning of the foetus. The preparatory stage lasts from 2 to 4 hours; when it ends the situation of the foal is usually as follows: its head is directed towards the vaginal opening; its back is uppermost; the fore-limbs are stretched beyond the foal's muzzle; the foetal membranes are as yet unbroken.

In the second stage the foal is expelled. It begins with rupture of the outer membrane and an escape of watery allantoic fluid that rinses the birth canal before running from the vagina (*Figure 6B*). The uterine contractions are now augmented by powerful strainings of the chest, belly, and diaphragm, which exert a strong backward force on the womb and foetus. (At this time the mare usually goes down on her side with legs extended.) Under these additional pressures, the inner membrane, tensely swollen with amniotic fluid, is forced into the birth canal and shortly appears at the vaginal opening. Straining continues and soon the forelegs may be seen inside the "water bag" usually with one foot in front of the other (*Figure 6C*). The "bag" ruptures and the head, shoulders and chest of the foal are squeezed through the vagina. At this time there may be a period of rest, after which the loins, hind limbs, and tail are expelled more quickly and with less effort. Although normally ruptured by the struggles of the foal, sometimes a tough package membrane fails to burst in which case it may be torn by an assistant. The arduous and decisive second stage, if uncomplicated, takes from 4 to 70 minutes, with durations between 10 and 30 minutes being most frequently recorded.

When does the newborn foal inhale its first breath? Probably when the head is uncovered and the nostrils detect the unfamiliar air. This may happen while the rump lingers in the birth canal and the umbilical cord is still intact. At the same moment the lungs inflate with air they receive a voluminous increase in their blood supply so that the special arterial by-pass—deprived of the blood now passing to the lungs—soon drops out of use, and the foramen ovale is blocked by the sealing up of its valve (*Figure 4C*). Respiration and heart function now gradually assume the adult patterns.

The main event of the third stage of parturition is expulsion of the foetal membranes as they loosen and separate from the uterine wall. When this happens, a good deal of valuable blood still in the membranes is squeezed by uterine contractions into the foal through

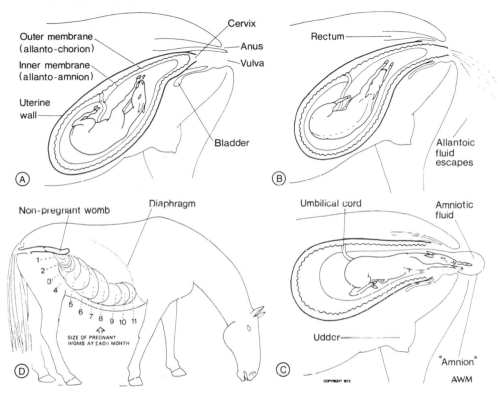

Figure 6 **A** *Parturition: intact package is squeezed by uterus to open birth canal; foetus upside down* **B** *Parturition: outer membrane bursts: foetus is turning* **C** *Parturition: amniotic bag swells out through vulva: foetus has turned and entered birth canal* **D** *Diagram showing approximate size of womb at each month of pregnancy. (In* **A, B,** *and* **C** *the foal is drawn disproportionately small to show membranes clearly. The mare, although usually recumbent, is shown standing for the same reason)*

the umbilical vessels. After this final transfusion the umbilical cord usually breaks (often as the mare gets up) leaving a stump on the foal's belly about 5 to 8 centimetres long. In normal births rupture of the cord should never be hastened or brought about artificially. A final bout of contractions throws out the membranes (now known as the afterbirth) and brings the third stage to a close after a duration of 30 minutes to 3 hours. When the discarded afterbirth is examined it is frequently seen to have been turned inside out; an arrangement facilitated by the foal's tugging on the umbilical cord before it breaks. If the membranes are unravelled, a hippomane may be found. The afterbirth is not normally eaten by the mare. From the opening of the birth canal to the casting out of the membranes, the total length of normal parturition varies between $2\frac{1}{2}$ and 8 hours.

The great majority of births occur at night and as befits the offspring of a running and grazing animal that has many natural enemies in the wild, the foal is set free in an advanced condition. Within a few hours or even minutes of birth, it is able to see and hear clearly, scent keenly, and move quickly—thanks to a long and thorough preparation in the womb.

GROWTH OF THE FOETAL HORSE IN LENGTH AND WEIGHT

Prenatal age in months	Length		Weight	
	cm	in.	g	lb.
1	1·0	0·4	1·0	·002
2	6·0	2·4	15·0	·03
3	14·0	5·5	150·0	·3
4	25·0	9·8	700·0	1·5
5	35·0	13·8	2000·0	4·4
6	50·0	19·7	5000·0	11·0
7	65·0	25·6	10000·0	22·0
8	80·0	31·5	16000·0	35·0
9	90·0	35·4	22000·0	48·0
10	100·0	39·4	30000·0	66·0
11	110·0	43·3	40000·0	88·0

The values given are only approximate and are based upon data from pregnant mares of about 1000 lb weight (450 kg). A useful but approximate rule for finding the age of a foetus from its length (X–X as indicated in Figure 3E) is:

$$2\tfrac{1}{2} \times \textbf{Length in centimetres} + 40 = \textbf{Age in days.}$$